C000085802

Cover illustration: The airship *L32* at Nordholz. The ship was making her thirteenth flight on the night that Werner Peterson and his crew of 21 perished when the 'Super Zeppelin' was set ablaze by Frederick Sowrey over Essex on 23/24 September 1916. *L32* was built in Freidrichshafen's Factory Shed No. 11 and made her maiden flight on 6 August. (F. Moch)

Air War over Great Britain

1914–1918

RAYMOND L. RIMELL

ARMS AND ARMOUR PRESS

Introduction

First published in Great Britain in 1987 by Arms and Armour Press Ltd., Link House, West Street, Poole, Dorset BH15 1LL.

Distributed in the USA by Sterling Publishing Co. Inc., 2 Park Avenue, New York, NY 10016.

Distributed in Australia by Capricorn Link (Australia) Pty. Ltd., P.O. Box 665, Lane Cove, New South Wales 2066.

British Library Cataloguing in Publication data
Rimell, Raymond L.
Air war over Great Britain, 1914–1918.
—(Vintage warbirds; 7)
1. World War, 1914–1918—Aerial operations, German 2. World War, 1914–1918.
—Campaigns—England
I. Title II. Series
940.4′42′0942 D604

ISBN 0-85368-804-4

Edited and designed by Roger Chesneau; typeset by Typesetters (Birmingham) Ltd.; printed and bound in Italy in association with Keats European Production Ltd., London.

◄2
1. (Title spread) A mixed assortment of BEs belonging to No.50 Home Defence Squadron: (from the left) BE2c 5778, BE2c 2711, a BE2e, BE2e A2767 and BE2c 4148; all, apart from 5778, are equipped for night flying. Piloting aircraft 2711 during the 2/3 September raid was Captain John Sowrey, who was forced to make an early return to his aerodrome at Dover with engine trouble. (J. M. Bruce/G. S. Leslie Collection)
2. One of the four Zeppelins brought down on British soil: the remains of *L48* at Theberton, Suffolk, 17 June 1917.

Most people are familiar with the Battle of Britain, when RAF Hurricane and Spitfire pilots defended Great Britain from the onslaught of Hitler's *Luftwaffe* during the sultry summer of 1940, yet now only a handful of senior citizens can recall the air battles that were fought in British skies a generation earlier when the 'Fathers of the Few' took on the Zeppelins and the Gothas in the First World War. The German bombing campaign began modestly enough with a lone attack on Dover by a small, two-seat floatplane in 1914, but initially at least it was the awesome Zeppelins that posed the greater threat with their capability for carrying a respectable weight of bombs over comparatively long distances. For the first time in history, British civilians were in the front line as the war was carried literally to their doorsteps by the *Kaiser*'s airships.

January 1915 saw the beginning of the Zeppelin raids, and for over a year the German Army and Naval Airship Divisions were able to embark on their nocturnal incursions with nothing to fear but the weather. It took time for British defences to evolve effectively, and, while searchlight and gun teams played their part, much was expected from the Home Defence squadrons of the Royal Flying Corps and Royal Naval Air Service which were being established around London, in the Home Countries and along the coast. Success eluded them for many months, and it was not until the latter part of 1916 that the tide was turned when five airships were brought down in flames by British pilots using newly developed incendiary ammunition.

Those British aeroplanes that had the performance to engage Zeppelins were simply not fast enough to catch the Gothas, and there was much public outrage as the raids continued virtually unopposed. Several squadrons were released from the Western Front as an interim measure while improved night-fighters were developed, and eventually the attacks ceased in 1918 – although this was due mainly to a more direct need for bombers in France where the situation was becoming increasingly more desperate for the German Army. Whilst it is true that the Home Defence squadrons had reached a high degree of effectiveness in the last year of the war, it ought not to be assumed that this represented a clear-cut victory over their opponents, and whilst it can be argued that the combined results of the German air raids on Great Britain were negligible by Western Front standards, and extremely costly to the Germans, the effort cannot be dismissed as a mere side-show, for a great number of men, materials and aeroplanes were withheld from France to combat the attacks.

It has not been easy to locate fresh photographs from the 'First Battle of Britain', but thanks to several helpful individuals supplementing the author's own collection even the best-read aero historian should find some surprises in the following pages; other readers, perhaps unfamiliar with recently published detailed works on the subject, will doubtless discover much that is new to them. As ever I am indebted to friends and colleagues for help with photographs, and I should like to express my thanks to the following: P. Amesbury; Mrs. A. J. Arkell; M. E. Bates; J. M. Bruce; Mrs. R. David; Sir Victor Goddard; the late P. L. Gray; Dr. V. Koos; G. S. Leslie; *Frau* Hertha Mathy; E. A. Munday; the Marine Luftschiffer Kameradschaft; Dr. D. H. Robinson; Sir Frederick Sowrey; and N. E. Tempest. All uncredited photos are from the Albatros Archive. Finally, I would like to dedicate this book to the memory of Captain William Leefe Robinson VC.

Raymond Laurence Rimell

▲3 ▼4

Air Raid on Colchester. Feb. 21st. 1915.

STANDING IN BOMB HOLE.

Officers Inspection

"DEBRIS"

WRECKED SHEDS

3. Friedrichshafen FF29 No.213. A machine similar to this, No.203 from *Seefliegerabteilung 1* of the German Navy, made the first airborne attack on Great Britain, dropping two bombs in the sea off Dover near Admiralty Pier on 21 December 1914. The FF29, from Zeebrugge, appeared off the coast at 1300 hrs. and was well on its way home before any defensive measures could be taken against it.

4. On 21 February 1915 another FF29 from *SFA 1*, flown by Stephan Prondzynski with observer *Fähnrich-zur-See* Heym, made a lone night attack, reaching Braintree where two incendiary bombs were dropped. On their return flight the airmen dropped a small HE bomb on Coggleshall and another near Colchester Barracks, damaging several buildings. This contemporary postcard shows the resultant damage.

5. On 14 April 1915 *Kapitänleutnant* Heinrich Mathy, one of the ablest airship commanders of the war, made a solo attack on Tyneside, where bombs from *L9* caused some damage at Wallsend. *L9* served as a training ship during September 1916 but on the 16th of that month she was destroyed in the Fuhlsbuttel shed by an inflation fire in *L6* (F. Moch)

6. The first ship from the German Army to attack Great Britain was *LZ38*, commanded by the redoubtable *Hauptman* Erich Linnarz, who bombed Bury St. Edmunds on the night of 29/30 April 1915. Some impression of the size of this Zeppelin can be gauged from the crew members manning the machine-gun post atop the forward hull – a precarious station by any standards. (D. H. Robinson)

▲7

7. *LZ38* over her base at Brussels-Evère, Belgium, in 1915. Under Linnarz's command *LZ38* took part in several successful raids and on the night of 31 May made the first ever aerial attack on London. Over a ton of bombs was dropped by *LZ38*, leaving seven civilians dead and a further 35 injured; damage to property exceeded £18,000, and not one of London's anti-aircraft guns engaged the raider. (D. H. Robinson)

8. Linnarz and the crew of *LZ38* adopt a striking pose. Linnarz was the Army's most successful airship commander, and he made a number of raids on Great Britain, surviving an attack on *LZ97* by Lt. W. L. Robinson of No.39 Home Defence Squadron on 25 April 1916. *LZ38*, London's first raider, was destroyed in its shed by RNAS airmen on 7 June 1915, the night Sub-Lt. R. A. J. Warneford brought down *LZ37* over Ghent. (D. H. Robinson)

9. On 7 June 1915 two Henry Farmans piloted by officers of 1 Squadron RNAS attacked the airship station at Brussels-Evère and succeeded in destroying *LZ38* in her shed. Flt. Lt. J. P. Wilson flew aircraft 3998 on this successful sortie, and the machine is seen here in the centre of this line-up. Both *LZ37* and *LZ38* had been returning from an abortive raid on Britain. (J. M. Bruce/G. S. Leslie Collection)

10. *L10* at Nordholz with the *Nobel* revolving shed and the smaller sheds *Nora* and *Norbert* in the far distance. This Zeppelin was the first Naval airship to bomb London, on 4 June 1915 under the command of *Kapitänleutnant* Klaus Kirsch. On 3 September *L10* was struck by lightning and fell blazing into the sea off Newark Island. None of her nineteen-man crew survived. (F. Moch)

▼8

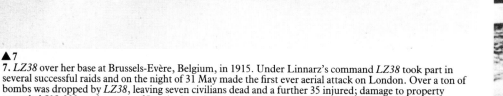

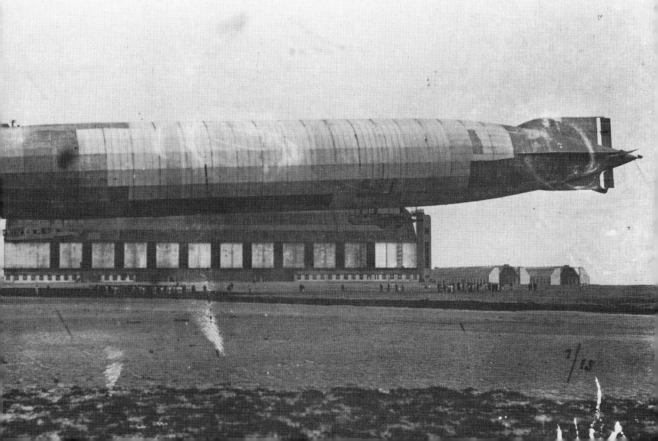

11. An abortive daylight raid on Harwich was made by an Albatros seaplane and a Gotha WD2 seaplane on 3 July 1915. Bombs dropped in the sea near Landguard Point signals station, but defending RFC and RNAS aeroplanes failed to make contact. This example of the WD was similar to the attacking machine from *SFA 1* at Zeebrugge. The unusual configuration provided a clear field of fire for the gunner.

12. The Type 'p' Zeppelin *L11*, which took part in the raid of 15 June 1915 but was forced to return early with engine trouble. *L11*, under *Kapitänleutnant* Buttlar, bombed Lowestoft on 9 August and took part in a number of subsequent raids with little effect until 5

March 1916 when, under *Korvettenkäpitan* Viktor Schutze, she successfully attacked Hull. In all, *L11* made eighteen raids, and she ended her days as a training ship. (Luftschiffbau Zeppelin)

13. During the 9 August raid *L12*, under the command of *Oberleutnant zur See* Werner Peterson, was struck by anti-aircraft guns from Dover and the subsequent rupturing of several gas cells forced the airship down into the Channel. At daybreak a German torpedo boat took *L12* in tow to Ostend, where various RNAS aeroplanes endeavoured to bomb the crippled airship. Although the attacks were unsuccessful, *L12* exploded when she was being hauled out of the water. (Luftschiffbau Zeppelin)

▲14

14. Seven civilians were killed and seven injured in the wake of an attack by *Oberleutnant zur See der Reserve* Friedrich Wenke's *L10* on Woodbridge in Suffolk. This is the corner of St. Johns Hill the following morning. Twenty-four bombs were dropped on Woodbridge during the attack and nearly seventy buildings were damaged or destroyed. (M. J. Taylor)

15. *L14* participated in seventeen raids, under *Kapitänleutnant der Reserve* Aloys Bocker, bombing Byland, Scarning and East Dereham on 8/9 September 1915 even though London was the intended target. On 23 June 1919 *L14* was deliberately 'scuttled' in the *Nora* shed at Nordholz by airship crews, thus denying her to the Allies. Several Zeppelins were destroyed in this way. *L14* is seen here passing the famous *Drehalle* in 1916. (F. Moch)

▼15

16. On 11/12 September 1915 *Hauptmann* Horn, commanding the Army ship *LZ77*, made a solo assault on London but, hampered by fog, dropped his entire load of sixty bombs on the RFA camp near North Weald Bassett, Essex. The safety pins had not been removed from the HE bombs, however, and none exploded. This contemporary postcard shows one of the recalcitrant HE bombs and three burnt-out incendiaries.

17. The last airship raid of 1915 took place on the night of 13/14 October and was particularly heavy, with 71 killed, 128 injured and many thousands of pounds worth of damage caused. Five airships set out from their bases to attack the capital, and *L14* dumped eighteen bombs on Croydon, where several private houses were wrecked. (M. E. Bates)

Presented by
"The Kaiser"
Septr 12th 1915

▲18 ▼19

18. *Kapitänleutnant* Joachim Breithaupt (*L15*) was the first to reach London on 13/14 October and dropped a salvo of bombs over London's 'Theatre Land' with devastating effect. Many casualties and considerable damage were left in the wake of the airship, which successfully evaded not only the few Home Defence aeroplanes sent up to intercept the raiders but also the mobile anti-aircraft gun at Finsbury. (M. E. Bates)

19. The control and forward engine cars of *L20*, which took part in the first airship raid of the New Year on 31 January 1916. Despite appearances there are actually *two* separate gondolas, but the gap is concealed with fabric. This two-car arrangement reduced the engine noise and vibration transmitted to the forward car and wireless cabin. (F. Moch)

20. On 9 February 1916 a daylight raid on Broadstairs and Ramsgate was made by a Friedrichshafen FF33e and a Hansa Brandenburg NW from *SFA 1*, Zeebrugge. Bombs dropped on Ramsgate narrowly missed a tramcar but a girls' school at Broadstairs was damaged by a stick of twelve missiles. Warnings were slow to reach Home Defence air stations and both raiders returned to their base unchallenged. Shown here is No.716, a typical FF33e.

21, 22. Another daylight raid took place on 19 March 1916, this time on Dover, Deal and Ramsgate. Six German machines took part, including Gotha Ursinus WD (*Wasser Doppeldecker*, or sea biplane) No.120 which, according to German reports, was the first machine to reach Dover, where 32 bombs were dropped. No.120 was the sole example built. Although both the RFC and RNAS mounted defensive patrols the Gotha went unseen by any British pilot in the air that day and neither did any of the many ground observers report sighting the big bomber. One of the raiders, FF33 No.537, was forced down by Flight Commander Bone RNAS in his Nieuport 10, serial 3964.

20▲

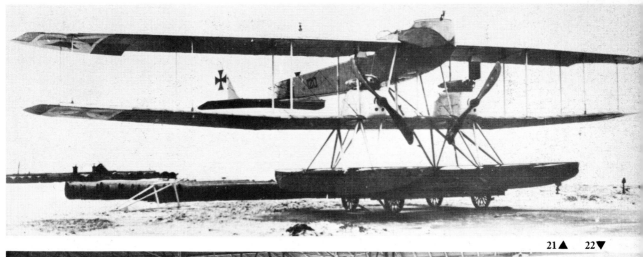

21▲   22▼

▲23

▼24

THE ZEP STRAFER

23. *L15*, under the command of Breithaupt, was lost during the 31 March 1916 raid following hits by anti-aircraft fire and concerted attacks by 2nd Lt. Alfred de Bathe Brandon in a BE2c of No.39 HDS from Hainault Farm, Essex. *L15* is seen here at Nordholz with the *Nora* and *Norbert* sheds in the background and the landing party already on the field. (F. Moch)

24. A contemporary 'cartoon' of Alfred de Bathe Brandon following his successful attack on *L15* which ended with the Zeppelin foundering off Margate sands and its crew being taken prisoner. Brandon also played a major role in the bringing down of the 'Super Zeppelin' *L33* which force-landed in Little Wigborough on 24 September 1916. (Brandon Family Archive)

25. A handful of French-built REP (Robert Esnault Pelterie) parasol monoplanes were operated by the RNAS on anti-Zeppelin patrols. This machine could be aircraft 8454, which flew from Eastchurch on 19 March 1916 during the daylight attack by *SFA 1*. The REP was powered by a Le Rhône rotary engine, and twelve were purchased by the RNAS. Note that the fuselage cockade lacks the usual white inner ring.

26. *LZ97* at Karlsruhe in 1916 with its hull number removed for security reasons. On 23/24 August Linnarz made a lone attack in this ship, bombing Trimley, Walton and Old Felixstowe, but the 34 bombs fell harmlessly on open fields. Although Royal Navy destroyer crews heard the Zeppelin's engines, *LZ97* was never once observed. (D. H. Robinson)

25▲ 26▼

▲27 ▼28

27. *LZ97* at Karlsruhe with the ground crew straining at the ropes; note the doped fabric patch obliterating the service numeral on the hull. *LZ97* took part in the fateful 2/3 September raid when one of the participating airships was brought down in spectacular fashion by a Home Defence pilot. (D. H. Robinson)

28. *Fregattenkäpitan* Peter Strasser received his *Pour le Mérite* award on 4 September 1917 from *Admiral* Scheer. Leader of Airships from October 1913 until his death aboard *L70* in August 1918, Strasser was held in high regard by his subordinates and truly led by example, rarely shirking from sharing the dangers of his men on active service. (Archiv Marine Luftschiffer Kameradschaft)

29. The officers of the German Naval Airship Division enjoyed comparatively lavish quarters and dining areas, many of the commanders living close by the stations with their wives and children. Some idea of the degree of comfort afforded them can be gauged from these well-appointed rooms at Nordholz. (P. Amesbury)

30. Airship commanders relaxing at the Hage base. Indicating a potential target is the youthful Werner Peterson, who was to meet his death over Billericay in the 'Super Zeppelin' *L32*; seated, left to right, are Joachim Breithaupt, Martin Dietrich and Heinrich Mathy. Mathy, too, would fall victim to the improved British defences after a successful career during which he was involved in many of the more effective bombing raids. (Bertha Dietrich via Peter Amesbury)

29▲   30▼

▲31 ▼32

31. The Holt wing-tip flare, seen here fitted to BE2c 2693, was a great aid to early night flying when introduced in early 1916. In those days such flying was extremely hazardous and a large number of experiments led to more efficient methods of illuminating airfields and identifying their true positions by a carefully coded system of lights. (J. M. Bruce/G. S. Leslie Collection)

32. A test installation of a 'Wing Tip Flare Mark H' fitted to a British Home Defence aeroplane. The crude sheet metal 'baffles' reduced the risk of blinding the pilot. The flare burned for 60 seconds and consisted of a wire lead which contained a fuse with a one-second delay. The leads were connected to the terminal at the top of the mounting and thence to the cockpit. (Public Records Office)

33. BE2c 2092, flown by 2nd Lt. Frederick Sowrey on the 24/25 August raid when thirteen airships left their bases with orders to 'attack England South'. Note the dark finish of this machine, and the forward cockpit faired over with a plain metal sheet. The photograph was taken in late 1916 at Suttons Farm as canvas hangars made way for more permanent wooden structures (right). (Sir Frederick Sowrey/RAF Museum)

34. BE2c 2693, at Eastchurch on 6 June 1916, reveals the upward-firing Lewis machine gun on the Strange mounting. Aircraft 2693 was flown by Lt. William Leefe Robinson on 2/3 September when he became a national hero literally overnight by shooting down the German Army's Schütte Lanz *SL11* during the largest airship raid yet mounted. (J. M. Bruce/G. S. Leslie Collection)

33▲   34▼

▲ 35

35. Sister-ship to *SL11*, and virtually identical in every respect, was *SL13*, a Type 'e' Schütte Lanz airship; she is seen here at Wittmundhaven on 20 October 1916. These wooden-hulled ships can quickly be distinguished from the more numerous metal-framed Zeppelins by their separate control and forward engine gondolas. (G. Blasweiler/D. H. Robinson)

36. Ground crewmen at Wittmundhaven reach up to catch the 'grab-rails' of *SL13* as she comes into land. Note the rippling of the thin control car windows and the ladders leading down from the hull to the cars. On the engine car on the left can be seen the retractable radiator and the ports (unglazed) through which crewmen could stave off fighter attacks with defensive machine guns. (G. Blasweiler/D. H. Robinson)

37. One of the many Zeppelins that embarked on the joint Army/Navy raid of 2/3 September 1916 was *LZ98*, seen here at Namur. *LZ98* was the first Army ship to reach London that night and dropped all her bombs over Tilbury. Lt. William Leefe Robinson encountered the Zeppelin at close quarters but he was unable to press home his attack as the airship escaped through cloud cover. (D. H. Robinson)

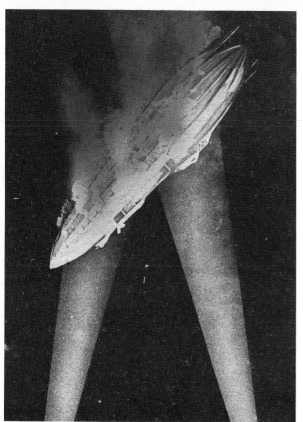

38. When Lt. W. L. Robinson brought down *SL11* the effect on British morale was enormous and the terrifying vision of the giant airship falling to earth wreathed in flames would remain in witnesses' memories all their lives. Many commemorative souvenirs appeared soon afterwards, including this picture postcard.

39. The morning after. The burning wreck of *SL11* fell near Castle Farm at Cuffley in Hertfordshire and the site was quickly swamped with sightseers, thousands of them swarming from London and its environs determined to see for themselves the results of Robinson's successful attack. Here, one of *SL11*'s engines – one of the few really large pieces of the ship left after the wreckage had burnt itself out – is being recovered. The entire crew of *SL11* perished and were subsequently buried at a small churchyard in nearby Potters Bar. Within 48 hours Robinson was awarded the Victoria Cross as a result of his action.

▲ 38   ▼ 39

40▲ 41▼

40. 'The man behind the gun'. Lt. W. L. Robinson seated in BE2c 2693 at Sutton's Farm, home of 'B' Flight, No.39 HDS. The airmen are holding the original centre-section of the aeroplane's upper wing damaged by Robinson's own gun during the attack on *SL11*. Some days later Robinson escaped unscathed when the famous aeroplane crashed on take-off and was burnt out. (Sir Frederick Sowrey)

41. On 23/24 September another airship fell to the defences when Lt. Frederick Sowrey of No.39 HDS brought down *L32* over Billericay, Essex. Like Robinson, Sowrey shot down the airship using the recently introduced incendiary bullets that were to exact such a toll on German airships in future months. Sowrey was awarded the DSO for the action.

▲42

42. Lt. Frederick Sowrey in the cockpit of aircraft 4112 at Suttons Farm. Note that the lower wing tips mount Holt flare brackets and that the front cockpit is faired over. The patches on the outer wing struts indicate the position of electrically operated Le Prieur rockets, which proved to be quite ineffective against airships and were quickly removed on active service. (N. E. Tempest)

43. Sowrey and his mechanics at Suttons Farm, September 1916.

The characteristic rippling of the laced-up fabric fuselage panel is evident, as is the strengthening of the undercarriage and centre-section struts by winding strips of fabric around and liberally doping them. This actual aeroplane is currently undergoing lengthy restoration work at the Canadian War Museum in Ottawa. (National Museum of Canada)

▼43

44 ▲

44. British officers visit Snail's Hall Farm at Great Burstead, near Billericay, where the burnt-out wreckage of *L32* lay in tangled heaps in the morning of 24 September. In the foreground is one of the propellers, together with its gear casing. The Zeppelin crewmen were buried at Great Burstead but in 1966 their remains, and those of other German dead from both World Wars, were re-interred at Cannock Chase. (E. A. Munday)

45. A Maxim machine gun lies in the wreckage of *L32* in the morning of 24 September. None of the Zeppelin's crew survived since parachutes were not standard issue for Naval airships and, though available, were shunned by the crews. Lifeboats were sometimes fitted in case of a forced descent into the sea but there is no record of them ever being deployed. (E. A. Munday)

45 ▼

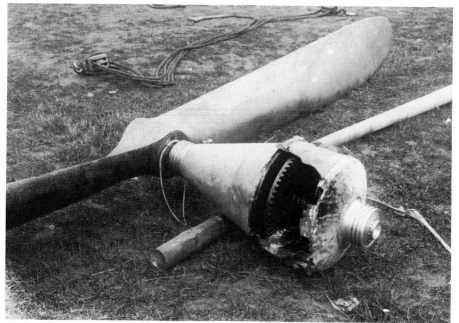

▲ 46   ▼ 47

46. The night *L32* was destroyed her sister-ship *L33* was forced to crash-land at Little Wigborough in Essex following attacks by Lt. Alfred Brandon and hits from accurate anti-aircraft fire which drained several gas cells. *L33* was virtually intact when it struck the ground and the crew were captured – quite a *coup* for British Intelligence. This is one of *L33*'s five giant propellers.

47. Lord French and staff officers study one of *L33*'s midships engine cars; note the fuel tanks at centre left. The crew of the Zeppelin, having set fire to their grounded vessel, were subsequently arrested by a local constable in circumstances which were almost farcical. Most of Böcker's men saw out the war in the Stobs POW camp. (E. A. Munday)

48. A photograph of what is thought to be one of the wicker, rubberized fabric-covered bumpers fitted beneath the port and rear cars of *L33* lying at Little Wigborough following the ship's dramatic force-landing on 24 September 1916. Two losses in one night constituted a severe blow to Strasser and his fellow officers, but, typically, this setback only served to strengthen their resolve. (E. A. Munday)

49. Shored up by scaffolding to prevent it collapsing, the nose of *L33* lies forlornly across Knapps Field, Little Wigborough, Essex. The British Admiralty spent many months measuring the wreck and recording details to such an extent that virtual copies were built, these being *R33* and *R34*, the former being completed in 1919 and broken up in 1928.

48▲ 49▼

50. The German Naval Airship Division suffered one of its severest blows on 1/2 October when *Kapitänleutnant* Heinrich Mathy, perhaps Strasser's most experienced officer, was killed aboard *L31*. The ship was brought down in flames over Potters Bar by Lt. Wulstan Tempest of 'B' Flight, No.39 HDS. Mathy is seen here in the control car of *L13*, his 'lucky ship'. (Archiv Marine Luftschiffer Kameradschaft)

51. Heinrich Mathy's last command, *L31*, being walked towards the *Normann* shed at Nordholz in July 1916. Two of the ship's lifeboats can be seen, one beyond the forward cars and another behind the upper gun platform. Hull numbers on Naval airships were prefixed with the letter 'L', while 'LZ' was adopted for all Army vessels. (*Frau Hertha Mathy*)

52. A Royal Navy tender (far right) takes away portions of the wrecked *L31* as a steady drizzle falls over Oakmere Farm, Potters Bar, on the morning of 2 October 1916. Despite the heavy military presence many souvenir hunters managed to obtain fragments of the metal structure. Mathy and his crew were buried at Potters Bar alongside the remains of *SL11* personnel. (E. A. Munday)

53. Posing in front of Robinson's aircraft, 2693, are 2nd Lts. C. C. Durston, F. Sowrey (*L32*) and W. L. Robinson VC (*SL11*); Capt. R. S. Stammers; and 2nd Lt. Wulstan Joseph Tempest, the pilot responsible for bringing down *L31*. 'B' Flight of No.39 HDS remained the most successful of the units pitched against the airship bombers. (Sir Frederick Sowrey)

▲50   ▼51

52▲   53▼

◀54

54. 2nd Lt. C. C. Durston stands before one of No.39 HDS's BE2e night-fighters. The BE2e was an 'improved' development of the BE2c and built in considerable numbers. It was not greatly superior to the earlier type but it remained in service until the Armistice, seeing out the war mainly as a trainer. (Mrs. R. David)

55. Another pose from the Durston family album. The BE2e, although fitted with flares for night flying, carries no armament, is retained as a two-seater and bears standard markings – from which one may assume that the machine was used as a night-flying trainer.

55▲

The single-bay, unequal-span wings distinguish this version from earlier BE types. (Mrs. R. David)

56. A rather formal study of German Naval Airship Division officers at Tondern. Identified are *Oberleutnant* Christian von Nathusius (left) and *Kapitänleutnant* Max Dietrich (third from left). Both men died in Dietrich's *L34* when it was shot down over the River Tees by 2nd Lt. Ian Pyott from 'A' Flight, No.36 Home Defence Squadron, on 27/28 November. (R. Frey/P. Amesbury)

56▼

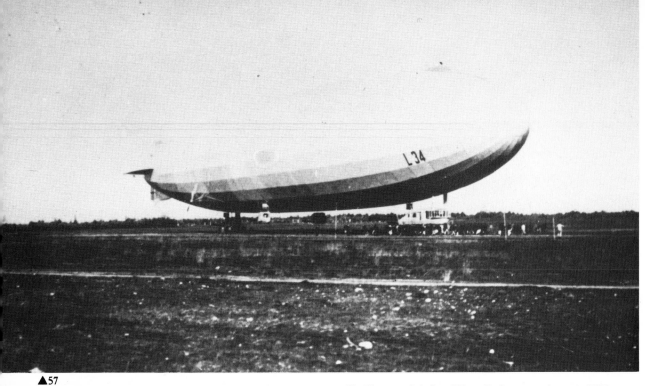

▲57
57. *L34* being walked into the *Normann* shed at Nordholz. Pyott was flying BE2c 2738 from Seaton Carew when he ended the careers of this Zeppelin and her entire crew during a night when two more Naval airships were lost. Pyott received the DSO for this action. (D. H. Robinson)

▼58

58. The second victim of Home Defence aeroplanes on 27/28 November was *L21*, under *Oberleutnant zur See* Kurt Frankenberg. The airship is seen here being walked into the revolving shed at Nordholz. The machine guns atop the hull are swathed in heavy jackets to protect them from the cold at high altitudes. (F. Moch)

59. Three RNAS BE2cs engaged *L21*, flown by Flt. Lt. Egbert Cadbury (8625) and Flt. Sub-Lts. Gerald W. R. Fane (8421) and Edward Pulling (8626). Although the last was credited with the Zeppelin's destruction it is generally accepted that Cadbury's initial attack sealed the raider's fate. This is Pulling's 8626 at Bacton. (P. Wright/J. M. Bruce/G. S. Leslie Collection)

60. Several hours after the German Navy lost two more airships *Leutnant* Walther Ilges and *Deckoffizier* Paul Brandt in LVG CVI 272/16 made a bold daylight attack on London. Although damage was slight the crew made their attack without opposition and the sortie was a portent of what was to follow. An LVG similar to that flown by Ilges and Brandt is shown here.

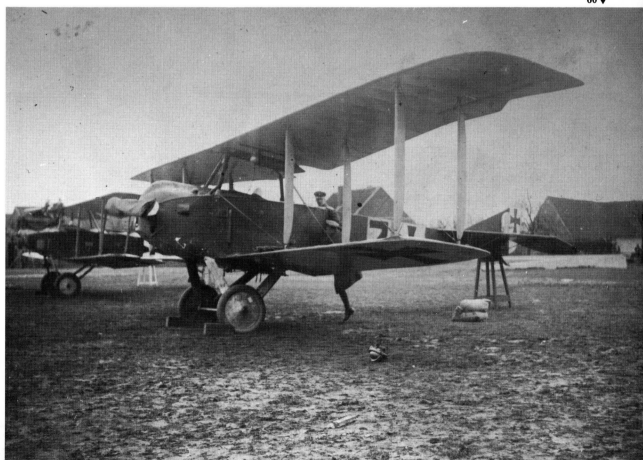

▲61

61. The BE2es of No.50 Home Defence Squadron were for a period painted 'Lamp Black' overall – including even the rear faces of their airscrews. National markings consisted of white rings in the standard positions. This crashed BE2e of No.50 HDS is partly painted in this manner, and the unit's emblem of a skull and crossbones is visible beneath the upper wing. (Mrs. A. J. Arkell)

62. A BE2e of No. 50 HDS, thought to be one of the six machines doped black overall as a result of a unit directive of 17 August 1916, 'partly for the sake of invisibility but mainly to prevent the pilot becoming blinded by the glare of his wing tip flares which he ignited when close to the ground'. (Mrs. A. J. Arkell)

▼62

63. Personnel of No.50 Home Defence Squadron pose with one of the unit's BE12 fighters; note the skull and crossbones device on the nose cowling. Such unit markings were not commonly seen on RFC machines – least of all those serving with Home Defence units. (Mrs. A. J. Arkell)

64. On 14 and 16 February 1917 a lone Sablatnig seaplane crewed by *Leutnant* Frantz and *Flugmeister* Elsasser made attacks on coastal shipping with no effect, but neither were Home Defence airmen any more successful for not one of them engaged the enemy. Shown here is a Sablatnig SF5 similar to the machine used in the first daylight attacks of 1917.

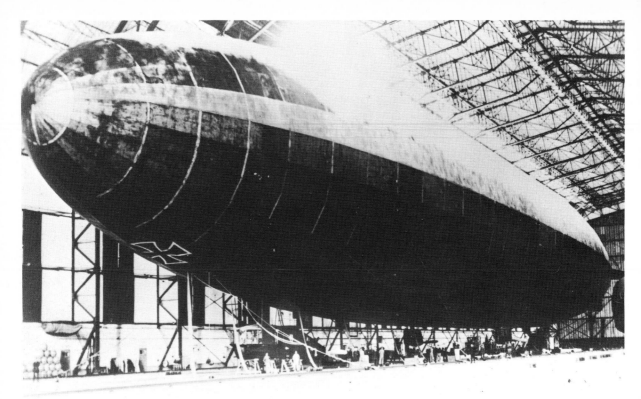

▲ 65

65. *L40*, with black dope applied to its undersides for camouflage, in the *Albrecht* shed at Ahlhorn. Under *Kapitänleutnant* Erich Sommerfeldt, *L40* took part in the largely abortive 16/17 March 1917 raid. The ship was one of several Type 'r' Zeppelins modified and lightened to reach higher altitudes in an endeavour to evade attacking aeroplanes. (Archiv Marine Luftschiffer Kameradschaft)

66. The unusual Robey Peters RRF 25 Mk. II was one of several aeroplanes designed primarily for use against airships. It was planned that the RRF would carry the Davis recoilless gun but only one example of the aeroplane was built. The prototype crashed on only its second flight and the pilot was lucky to escape from the cockpit, which was unusually positioned well aft of the wings.

▼ 66

67▲

67. The gradual attrition of airships and their valuable crews due to the improved British defences resulted in a reduction in the number of Zeppelin raids in favour of attacks mounted by aeroplanes, and the Gotha twin-engined bomber, and later the Giant 'R-Planes', proved to be a far deadlier threat. The Gotha GIII saw service on the Western Front and proved extremely effective. (Dr. V. Koos)

68. On 25 May 1917 twenty-one Gothas attacked Folkestone, taking British defences completely by surprise. Ninety-five civilians were killed and 195 injured as the bomber fleet wheeled over the target and then returned safely to its base virtually unopposed. The Gotha GIVs taking part in this raid were similar to the one depicted.

68▼

▲ 69   ▼ 70

69. A 'mint' example of a Gotha GIV reveals its well-proportioned lines. Bomb racks can be seen beneath the nose and rear fuselage, with slots on the lower wing centre-section for the internally mounted bombs which were held in vertical racks. The Gothas were well armed, carrying a nose gunner and a rear gunner who could fend off attacks from below thanks to the machine's fuselage gun tunnel.

70. Gotha GV 604/17. The GV was lighter and stronger than the GIV and initial production machines reached the first squadrons in August 1917. Both GIVs and GVs were used in the daylight and later night attacks with great effect, and defending pilots found them difficult to shoot down. For a large aeroplane, the Gotha was surprisingly agile.

71. Despite the improved defences, Strasser despatched six airships on 16 June 1917 to bomb London. Among the raiders was *L48* (under *Kapitänleutnant der Reserve* Franz Eichler), one of the few to reach English shores. But *L48* was doomed. She was attacked by at least three British aeroplanes, the *coup de grace* being delivered by Lt. L. Watkins flying BE12a 6610 from No.37 HDS. (Luftschiffbau Zeppelin)

71▼

72. The wreckage of *L48* fell in a field at Theberton, Suffolk, and the following morning the RNAS took charge. On the left can be seen the floor of the upper gun platform. Miraculously there were three survivors from the Zeppelin, although one would die of his injuries several months later. See also photograph 2. (Sir Victor Goddard)

73. A BE12 night-fighter. Note the rocket rails on the outboard interplane struts and the Mk. IV gun mounting angled upwards for anti-Zeppelin attack. It was in a machine similar to this that Canadian-born Lt. Loudon P. Watkins attacked *L48* over Theberton in June. (J. M. Bruce/G. S. Leslie Collection)

74. Lewis guns mounted to the centre section of a BE12 from an unidentified Home Defence squadron. Note the ring sight clamped to the rear starboard strut and the heavy rippling of the laced-up fuselage panel. The forward cockpit area has been filled with a purpose-made petrol tank to increase the aircraft's operational endurance. (Sir Frederick Sowrey)

74 ▶

▲72 ▼73

▲ 75

75. The first commander of Gotha squadron *Kagohl 3* was
Hauptmann Ernst Brandenburg and shown here are machines from
that unit. Although the photograph is of poor quality, it may be
seen that the second machine at left has a dark tail and a 'hunting
horn' marking on the rear fuselage. Such personal devices on Gotha
bombers were rare.

76. Even in 1917 night flying was still hazardous, witness this
unfortunate BE12. Of interest here are the national markings,
where the white areas of the wing cockades and rudder have been

overpainted to assist camouflage. The circumstances and location of
this accident are not known, nor is the identity of the unit involved.
(J. M. Bruce/G. S. Leslie Collection)

77. Twenty of the twenty-one Gothas on their return from the 7 July
raid on London. For the second time the German raiders were to
encounter relatively light opposition: only twenty British aeroplanes
engaged the bombers on their return, and they succeeded in
bringing down one of the Gothas.

▼ 76   77▶

 ▲78 ▼79

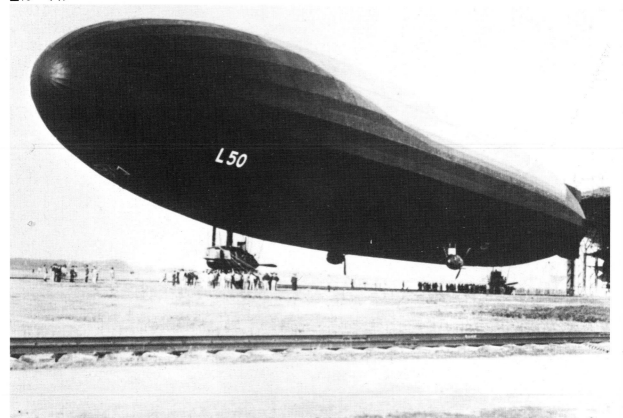

78. *L46*, having just landed at Ahlhorn, 14 June 1917. This airship took part in the abortive raid of 21/22 August and the more costly attack of 19/20 October when the so-called 'Silent Raid' resulted in the loss of five airships due to adverse weather at lofty altitudes. *L46* was subsequently destroyed in a mysterious hangar fire at Ahlhorn on 27 December. (F. Frey/P. Amesbury)

79. Another casualty of the 'Silent Raid' was *L50*, which was lost out to sea following attacks by French aeroplanes and anti-aircraft fire after the raiders had been blown across France by gales. Seventy-eight Home Defence sorties were mounted against the raiders but few pilots were able to locate the airships let alone engage them. (Luftschiffbau Zeppelin)

80. A Home Defence BE12 fitted with an impressive armament of three overwing Lewis guns and a fourth mounted forward of the cockpit; what effect this weighty ordnance had on the machine's performance can only be imagined. Also of interest here are the exhaust pipes, which have had their extension tubes removed. (Mrs. A. J. Arkell)

81. Gotha GV 937/16, photographed in September 1917; note the 'cloud' marking on the nose. On 3/4 September the Germans switched to night attacks, with four Gothas dropping bombs over the Chatham naval base, Sheerness and Margate. One hundred and thirty-two people were killed and 96 injured as a result of this attack.

◀80

81▼

▲82

82. Another *Kagohl 3* Gotha in full night-bomber camouflage. The armourers are installing 50kg PUW bombs to the wing racks while a pair of 100kg PUWs are suspended from the centre-section. Note the cables and throttle controls running from the fairing down to the lower wing.

83. On 28/29 September the Giant *Riesenflugzeuge* ('R-Planes') were

used to attack Britain in company with 25 Gothas, although bad weather all but caused a débâcle. Nevertheless the Giants were to prove effective weapons and none was ever brought down by Home Defence pilots. This example is an Aviatik-built RVI, the most numerous of the 'R-Plane' designs.

▼83

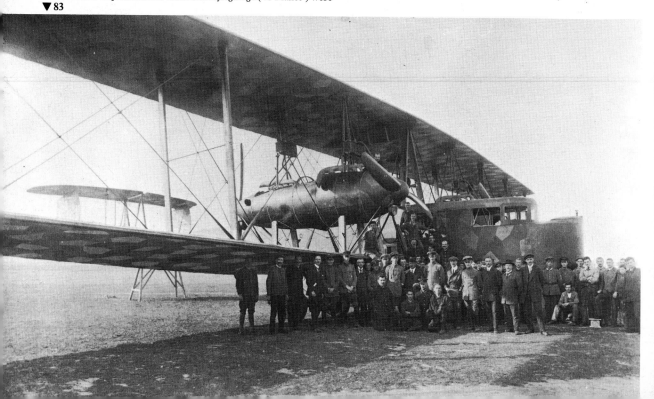

84. Twenty-five Gothas and three 'R-Planes' were despatched for a raid on 28/29 September but owing to adverse weather only three bombers pressed home the attack. Six Gothas crashed due to malfunction or bad landings and one of these, GIV 602/16, is seen in this photograph at Ghent the following day. Note the 'serpent' adorning the fuselage sides.

85. Another GV fully bombed up for a raid on London. At the rear of the centre-section pylons can be seen a wire mesh safety guard to prevent crew members from being struck by the pusher propellers, the tips of which were in close proximity to the fuselage.

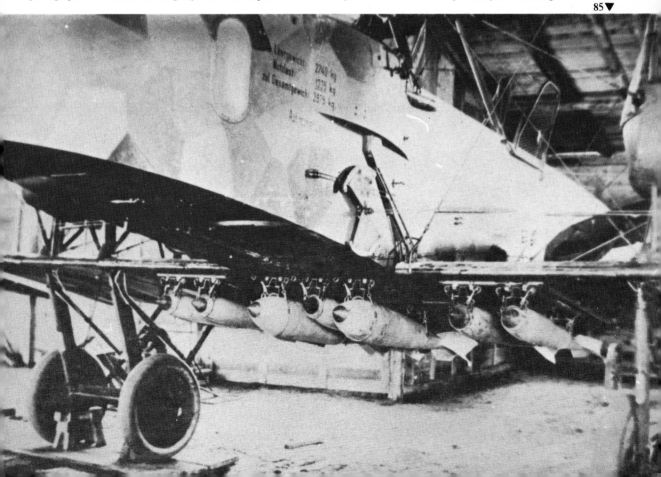

▲86   ▼87

50

86. The nose gunner of a Gotha GVa demonstrates the downward-firing capability of his Parabellum machine gun. Many Gothas were lost in landing accidents and nose wheels were fitted to later aircraft in a bid to prevent such mishaps; mounted on this machine is the *Stossfahrgestell* developed by the Siemens Schuckert Werke.

87. A Gotha GV crew pose belligerently at their stations. The fuselage marking bears evidence of repainting to convert the original *croix pâtée* into the later, straight-sided form. The aeroplane is camouflaged overall in one of the many polygonal lozenge patterns used extensively by the Germans in the latter years of the First World War.

88. The pilot's cabin of a typical 'R-Plane' (in this case an RVI) was comfortable and roomy by the standards of the day. At right centre is the fold-down navigator's table, and two of the fuel tanks can be seen at either side of the photograph. Note the central door between the control wheels for access to the nose gunner's position.

89. R26, under construction, reveals details of its capacious bomb bay. Most Giants were capable of carrying three times the warload of the Gothas and were to cause some of the greatest casualties meted out by German bombers in the First World War. Note the modern-looking hanging bomb doors.

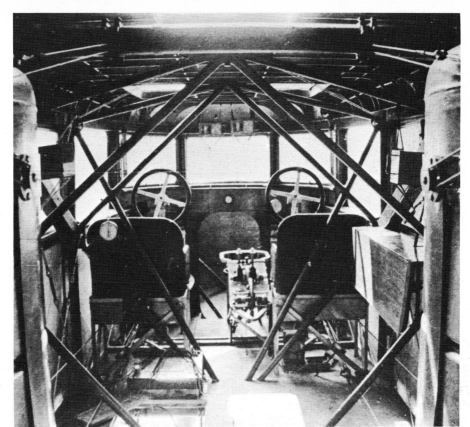

88 ▲   89 ▼

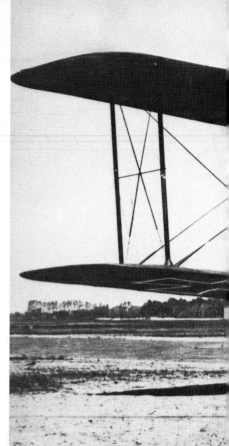

▲90　▼91

90, 91. Two unusual views of Staaken RVI No. R26/16, both taken from the gunner's cockpit. In photograph 90 the machine has just taken off and the pilot has slid open his side window for the photographer to obtain a clearer image; photograph 91 provides an impressive view of the port engine nacelle housing its two powerful Mercedes DIVa motors and an in-flight engineer. In later aeroplanes, a gun position was installed in the upper wing and could be reached from the nacelle by ladder.

92. A typical Staaken RVI, serial unknown. The man by the nearest ladder gives some impression of the enormous size of these aeroplanes, which boasted an average wing span some 40ft greater than that of the Avro Lancaster of the Second World War. Note the overall camouflage, which was hand-painted on these machines.

93. Another Zeppelin Staaken RVI, undergoing maintenance. These giant bombers were operated by *Rfa 501*, stationed around Ghent in Belgium. Eighteen RVIs were eventually built (R25–39 and R52–54), six by Aviatik, seven by Schütte Lanz and four by OAW. R25 scored a direct hit on St. Pancras station during a daring solo attack in February 1918.

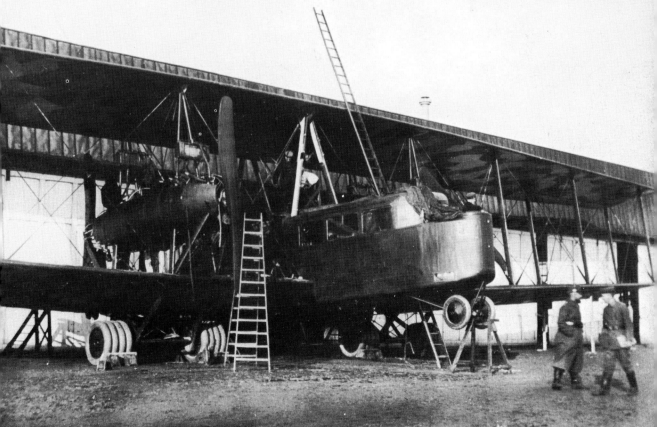

▲94

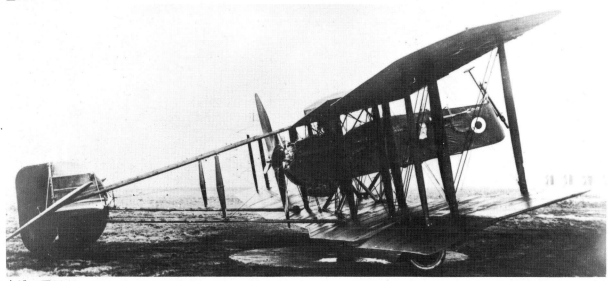

▲95 ▼96

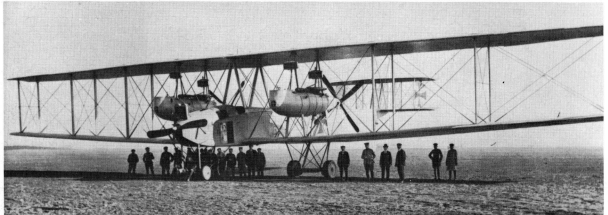

94. A BE12 of 'D' Flight, No.39 Home Defence Squadron, based at Biggin Hill in late 1917. The machine lacks night camouflage but is fitted with Holt flares. The white outer ring to the lower wing cockades is of interest. (Mrs. A. J. Arkell)

95. The Night-Flying Experimental No. 1 was developed from the Royal Aircraft Factory's FE12 and first flew on 8 September 1917. Six prototypes were built and here is the first, B3971, at Martlesham Heath in full night camouflage. Note the Crayford rocket gun mounted on the forward cockpit. The NF1 was not adopted for service, more reliance being placed on standard, proven types modified for night flying.

96. Staaken RIV No.12/15 was one of the more successful of the 'R-Planes' and, indeed, was to enjoy an operational life longer than that of any other Giant. R12's first appearance over Britain was during the 18/19 December 1917 raid when it dropped incendiaries and a pair of 660pdrs on London. Thirteen Gothas also took part, one being damaged and brought down after an attack by a Camel flown by Capt. G. W. Murlis Green.

97, 98. R12 later in its career. At this stage the machine had been camouflaged, and later still the white-outline *croix pâtées* were painted out to make way for the straight-sided *Balkenkreuze* as seen here. On 16/17 February 1918 four Giants attacked London and Dover, including R12 which had a lucky escape when its starboard wing struck the London balloon apron necessitating a rapid recovery from the pilot *Leutnant* Golte. Little damage was done and R12 went on to bomb Beckenham. The in-flight view shows the engineer mounting the steps to one of the upperwing gun stations.

97 ▲　98 ▼

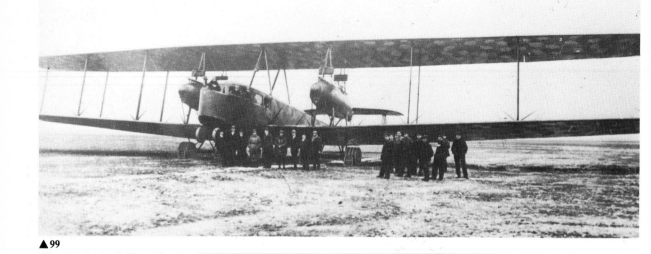

▲99

▲100 ▼101

99. Staaken RVI R33 also took part in the 16/17 February raid, despite suffering serious engine problems; its bombs were hastily dropped on warships at Deal in an effort to lose weight. Thanks to an enterprising mechanic who kept the rear port engine going by transferring oil by hand, the Giant managed to reach its base at Scheidewidecke safely.

100. Another purpose-designed night-fighter that failed to meet expectations was the Vickers FB26. B1484 was completed by December 1917 and this machine went to Martlesham Heath, where it is seen in this photograph armed with three Lewis guns on an Eeman triple mounting. Named 'The Vampire', B1484 went to No.141 HDS at Biggin Hill in early 1918 for operational evaluation.

101. Zeppelin Staaken RVI R39 took part in five attacks on Britain and dropped the first 1,000kg bomb during the 16/17 February raid and a second on the night of 7/8 March when several houses in Warrington Crescent, Maida Vale, were demolished and a further

nineteen damaged. These were the largest bombs dropped on Britain during the First World War.

102. One of many defending aeroplanes aloft during the night of 17/18 February 1918 when R25 made its effective solo raid was SE5a B658 of No. 61 HDS. Flown by Capt. C. A. Lewis, it was struck accidentally by AA fire but landed safely. The aeroplane is seen here later in the war with an experimental colour scheme applied to the uppersurfaces.

103. The superb Bristol F2B Fighter served with several Home Defence units, notably No.39 HDS. Three machines from this squadron are seen at North Weald. The aeroplane in the centre is C4650, flown by Captain J. M. Clarke who, on the night of 16/17 February, attacked another No.39 HDS F2B in error – fortunately without result. The variety of markings may be noted. (Mrs. A. J. Arkell)

103 ▼

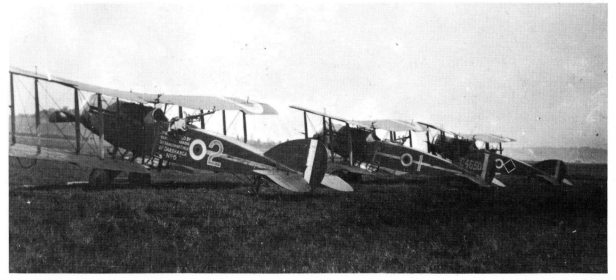

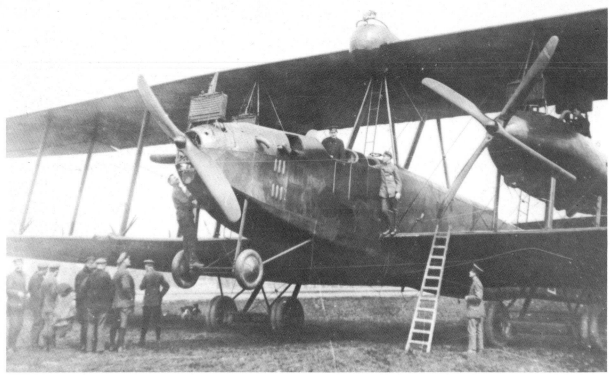

▲ **104**

104. On 19/20 May 1918 28 Gothas and one 'R-Plane' attacked London, other raiders dropping bombs over Essex and Kent. R13 failed to penetrate very far. This RV reveals many differences compared with later aeroplanes in the series although the wing cellules of most Staakens remained the same. Note the upperwing centre-section pulpit carrying a gunner who enjoyed an uninterrupted field of fire.

105. From the British pilot's point of view the 19/20 May raid was a significant one. This is Bristol F2B C4636, of No.39 HDS, flown by Lt. A. J. Arkell, with First Air Mechanic A.T.C. Stagg as gunner,

who brought down one of the Gothas over East Ham. This Bristol was nicknamed 'Devil in the Dusk' by its pilot. (Mrs. A. J. Arkell)

106, 107. The remains of Arkell and Stagg's Gotha on waste ground rear Roman Road, East Ham. Recognizable are one of the engine nacelles, a propeller and the main undercarriage units. Two members of the Gotha's crew, *Vizefeldwebel* Hans Thiedke and Paul Sapkowiak, jumped to their deaths before the bomber struck the ground, while *Gefreiter* Wilhelm Schulte was killed in the crash. (Mrs. A. J. Arkell)

▼ **105**

106 ▲ 107 ▼

▲108 ▼109

110▲

108. Lt. L. Lucas, of No. 50 HDS, made no contact with any of the 19/20 May raiders while patrolling in SE5a D5995. Note the absence of fuselage cockades on this machine and the painted band and numeral. The ends of the exhausts are covered with special flame-damping baffles, in order to reduce the effects of glare on pilots' night vision. (Mrs. A. J. Arkell)

109, 110. Another Gotha was brought down on 19/20 May following attacks by Maj. Frederick Sowrey of No.143 HDS flying an SE5a and Lts. Edward Turner and H. B. Barwise in Bristol Fighter C851. The Gotha GV, serial 979/16, crashed between Frinstead and Harrietsham. It was fitted with the SSW nose wheels and bore the

letters 'FST' on its fuselage, indicating the crew's initials: *Leutnant* Joachim Flathow (killed); *Vizefeldwebel* Albrecht Sachtler (killed); and the only survivor, *Unteroffizier* Hermann Tasche. (Sir Frederick Sowrey)

111. BE12b, of No.141 HDS, which was flown by Capt. N. H. Dimmock on 17/18 February 1918 during R25's dramatic attack on London when almost £40,000 worth of damage was caused. The BE12b was powered by the Hispano-Suiza engine which made this version easily distinguishable from earlier BE types. (J. M. Bruce/ G. S. Leslie Collection)

111▼

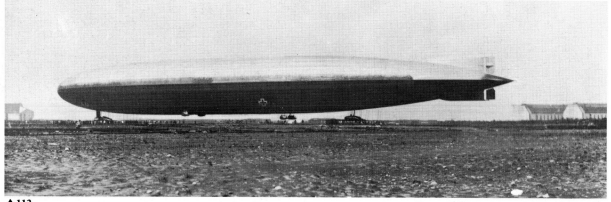

▲112

112. On 5/6 August 1918 Strasser personally conducted a raid aimed at the Midlands and thanks to a mixture of miscalculation and foolhardy disregard for the defences his force arrived over the coast before nightfall. Strasser was flying in the latest Zeppelin, *L70*, which is believed to have been armed with Becker cannon for defence. If so, these failed to save *L70*, which fell in flames after attacks by a DH4 from Yarmouth. (Luftschiffbau Zeppelin)
113. The RAF airmen who successfully attacked *L70* were Majors Egbert Cadbury and Robert Leckie, flying a De Havilland DH4. This is believed to be the aeroplane they flew that evening when they effectively dealt the final blow to the German Naval Airship Division. Following the death of Strasser, never again did German airships raid Great Britain. (P. Cadbury)

114. One of many machines aloft on the night of 5/6 August 1918 was this BE12b, C3094, flown by Lt. W. E. Watt of 'A' Flight, No.76 HDS, from Copmanthorpe. During his patrol Watt came under fire from AA positions, as did other BE12bs and several Bristol fighters, but no aeroplane was struck. (Mrs. A. J. Arkell)
115. At first it was thought that the Sopwith Camel, often difficult to manage in normal circumstances, would be totally unsuitable for night-flying. However, during the 3/4 September 1917 night raid, Capt. G. W. Murlis Green of 'C' Flight, No. 44 HDS, and two fellow-pilots proved that the frisky Camel could be flown safely on night patrols. (Mrs. A. J. Arkell)

▼113

▼114   115▶

▲116

116. Another Bristol F2B fighter of No. 39 HDS. The mercurial Bristol ultimately proved itself as one of the most successful of the night-fighters, and several 'Biff' crews were responsible for bringing down Gothas during the night raids. (Mrs. A. J. Arkell)

▼117

117. The Staaken RIV R12/16 and its crew at Kassel after the war. The total weight of bombs dropped by this single machine on the targets aimed at has been chalked on the fuselage side. R12 was broken up in April 1919 after a long and eventful career.

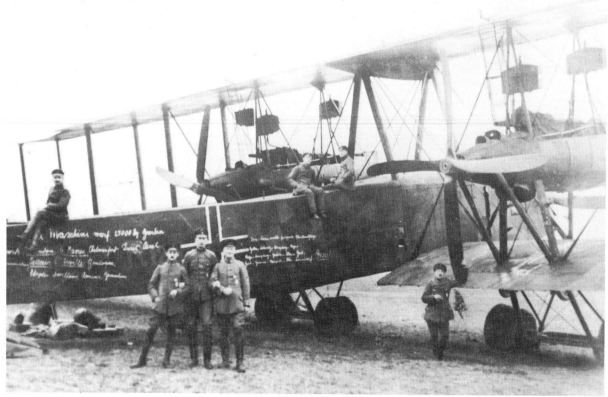